All About Dinosaurs

Pterodactyl

Daniel Nunn

Heinemann
LIBRARY
Chicago, Illinois

T0052511

© 2015 Heinemann Library
an imprint of Capstone Global Library, LLC
Chicago, Illinois

To contact Capstone Global Library, please call 800-747-4992, or visit our web site www.capstonepub.com

All rights reserved. No part of this publication may be reproduced or transmitted in any form or by any means, electronic or mechanical, including photocopying, recording, taping, or any information storage and retrieval system, without permission in writing from the publisher.

Edited by Daniel Nunn and James Benefield
Designed by Tim Bond
Picture research by Tracy Cummins
Production by Helen McCreath
Originated by Capstone Global Library Ltd

Library of Congress Cataloging-in-Publication Data
Nunn, Daniel, author.
Pterodactyl / Daniel Nunn.
pages cm.—(All about dinosaurs)
Includes bibliographical references and index.
ISBN 978-1-4846-0205-8 (hb)—ISBN 978-1-4846-0212-6 (pb) 1. Pterodactyls—Juvenile literature. I. Title.

QE862.P7N86 2015
567.918—dc23 2013040466

Acknowledgments
We would like to thank the following for permission to reproduce photographs: age footstock p. 10 (© fotototo); Alamy pp. 8 (© Stocktrek Images, Inc.), 21(© Corbin17); Corbis p. 18 (© Kevin Schafer); Getty Images pp. 7 (Andrew Kerr), 23 (Ulrich Baumgarten); istockphoto p. 5 (© johan63); Photoshot p. 15 (Raymon Tercafs); Science Source pp. 13 (Roger Harris), 20 (Tom McHugh); Shutterstock 5a (Michael Rosskothen), 5b (Matt Jeppson), 5c (Cathy Keifer), 7 background (mycola), 9 (Space-kraft), 11, 12, 14 (Michael Rosskothen), 16 (Vlada Zhykharieva), 23 (tratong); Superstock pp. 4 (Stocktrek), 6 (Science Photo Library), 17 (Stocktrek Images), 19 (Universal Images Group).

Cover photograph of three Pteranodon Longicepts flying, with two diplodocus dinosaurs near the shore, with permission of Shutterstock (Linda Bucklin).

Back cover photograph of pterodactyl reproduced with permission of Shutterstock (Michael Rosskothen).

We would like to thank Dee Reid and Nancy Harris for their invaluable help in the preparation of this book.

Every effort has been made to contact copyright holders of material reproduced in this book. Any omissions will be rectified in subsequent printings if notice is given to the publisher.

Printed in the United States 5648

Contents

Meet the Pterodactyls 4
What Were Pterodactyls Like? 8
Where Are Pterodactyls Now? 16
Where in the World? 22
Picture Glossary 23
How to Say It 23
Index 24
Notes for Parents and Teachers . . .24

Meet the Pterodactyls

Pterodactyls lived long ago.
They are also called pterosaurs.

Pterodactyls were reptiles.
Snakes, crocodiles, and lizards
are reptiles that live today.

Some pterodactyls were big.
Pteranodon was big.

There were other types of pterodactyls. Pterodactylus was small.

What Were Pterodactyls Like?

Pterodactyls had wings.

Pterodactyls could fly.

Pterodactyls had four legs.

Pterodactyls could walk.

Pterodactyls had long beaks.

Pterodactyls ate fish, insects, and small animals.

Some pterodactyls had teeth.

Some pterodactyls did not have teeth.

Where Are Pterodactyls Now?

Pterodactyls are extinct. There are no pterodactyls alive now.

All the pterodactyls died long ago.

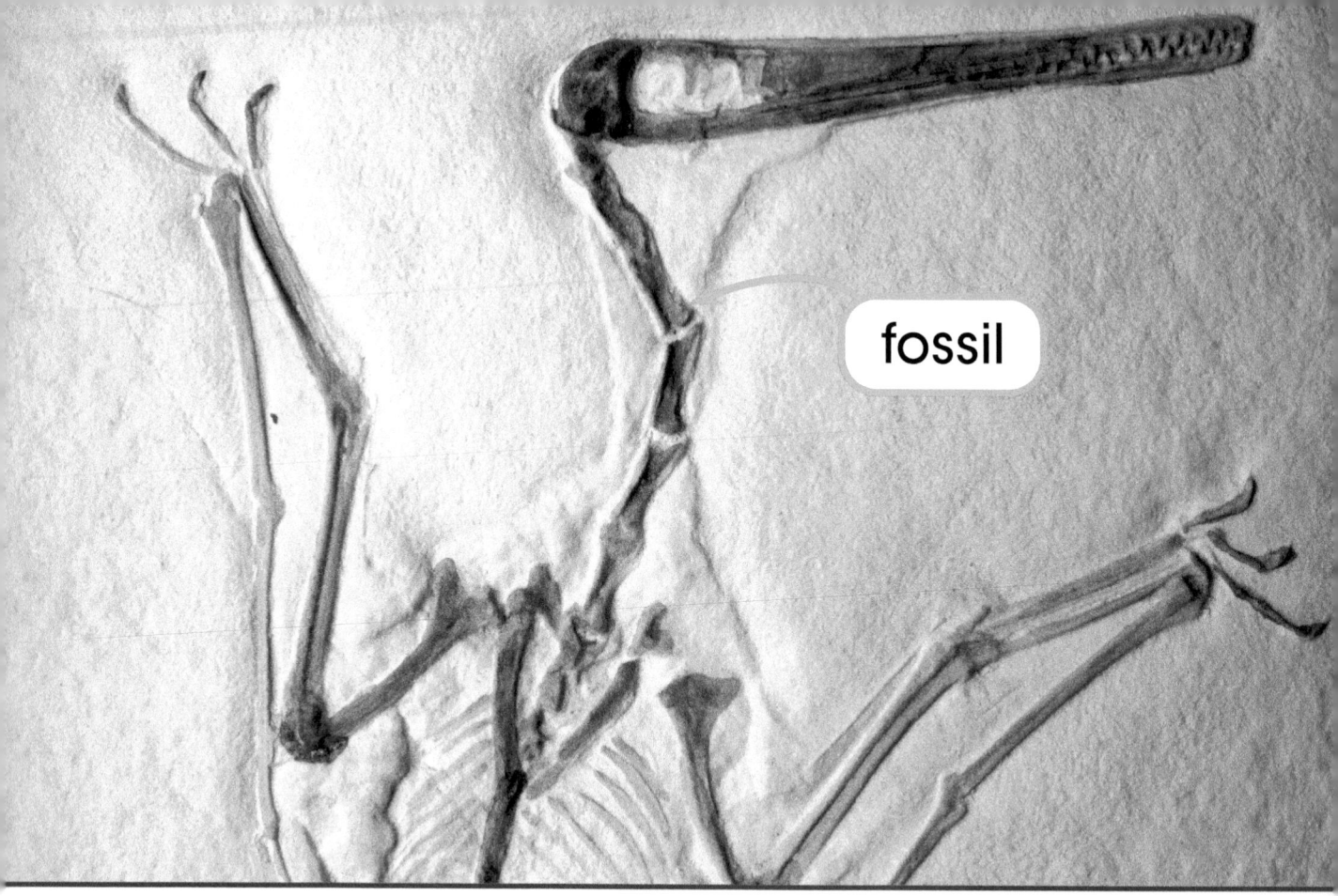

We learn about pterodactyls from fossils.

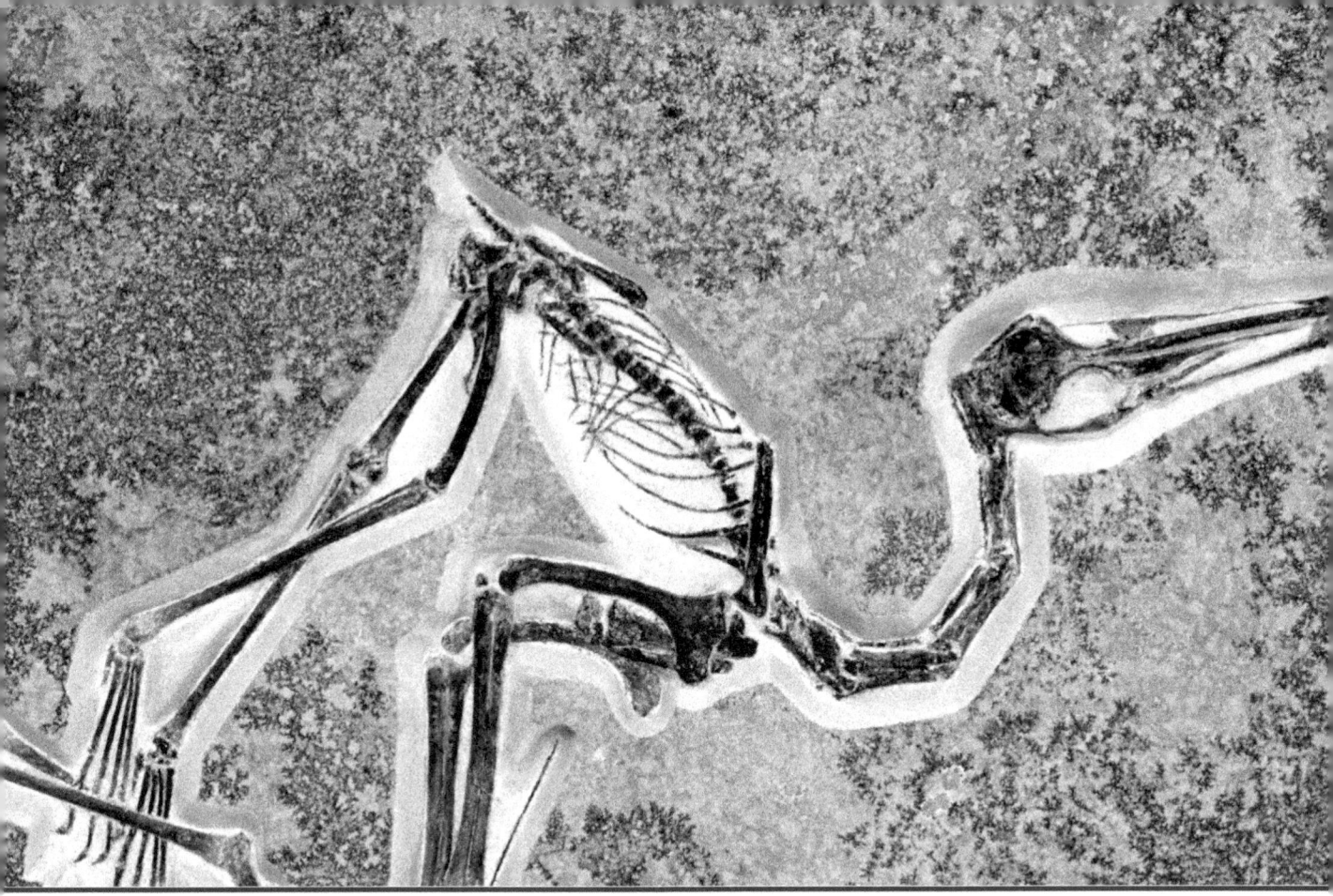

Fossils are animal bones that have turned to rock.

People find fossils in the ground.

Fossils show us what pterodactyls looked like.

Where In the World?

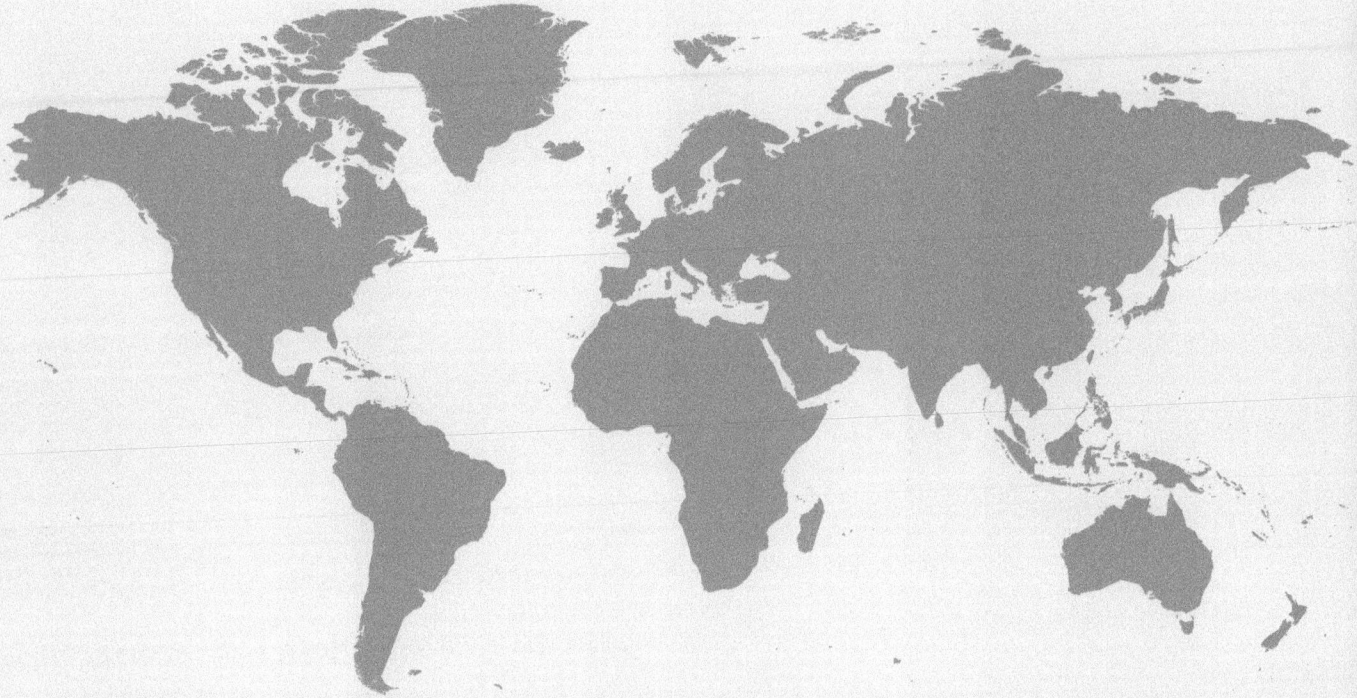

Pterodactyl fossils have been found all over the world.

Picture Glossary

fossil animal bones or parts of a plant that have turned into rock

reptile cold-blooded animal. A lizard is a reptile.

How to Say It

Pteranodon: say "terr-arn-uh-don"

Pterodactyl: say "terr-uh-dak-til"

Pterodactylus: say "terr-uh-dak-til-us"

Index

beaks 12
crocodiles 5
fossils 18–21, 22, 23
lizards 5
reptiles 5, 23
snakes 5
teeth 14–15
wings 8

Notes for Parents and Teachers

Before Reading

Ask the children to name some dinosaurs. Ask them if dinosaurs are around today. Have they heard of pterodactyls? Explain that pterodactyls were not dinosaurs, but they lived at the same time as dinosaurs. Find out if they already know about pterodactyls.

After Reading

- Choose some fast music and ask the children to fly like pterodactyls. Show them how to flap their arms and then hold them still as they glide. Ask the children to imagine they are diving to catch a fish. Then ask them to walk like a pterodactyl on the land.
- Ask the children to draw pterodactyls flying with outstretched wings. Get them to cut out their drawings and hang them from the classroom ceiling, so that they fly above the children's heads.